A Method,
A Path

Also by Rowan Evans

The Last Verses of Beccán

Penguin Modern Poets 7: These Hard and Shining Things

A Method, A Path

ROWAN EVANS

BLOOMSBURY POETRY

LONDON · OXFORD · NEW YORK · NEW DELHI · SYDNEY

BLOOSMBURY POETRY
Bloomsbury Publishing Plc
50 Bedford Square, London, WC1B 3DP, UK
29 Earlsfort Terrace, Dublin 2, Ireland

BLOOMSBURY, BLOOMSBURY POETRY and the Diana logo
are trademarks of Bloomsbury Publishing Plc

First published in Great Britain, 2023

A catalogue record for this book is available from the British Library

ISBN: PB: 978-1-5266-5122-8; eBook: 978-1-5266-5125-9;
ePDF: 978-1-5266-5124-2

2 4 6 8 10 9 7 5 3 1

Typeset by Laura Jones
Printed and bound in Great Britain by
CPI Group (UK) Ltd, Croydon CR0 4YY

To find out more about our authors and books
visit www.bloomsbury.com and sign up for our newsletters

ON ĒGLOND

I

Listen.

It's as if someone offers you a message.
Do you receive me?

The transmission interrupted by crows,
growing dark bristles and claws.

The song swallowed by a sinkhole,
then thrown up after centuries
as mutterings of a bog-queen.

The dispatch intercepted by a cold wind,
snagged on too many thorns.

Torn up, chewed on, translated, left for dead.

Gehȳrest þū ?

II

I want to talk to you, but the books
thickness to it, like reading each page
words whose letters keep growing
thicket. Running a finger along þese
skin, cutting it. A little blood, ink,
a page in a book and start seeing þe
streams and rills, coiling down þe
become dull blocks of shadow. Have you
a language you don't understand? Þe
landscape sinking under rising flood.
island of lines with a white cut down
shift and the river bends.   Þe
separated, have been severed, but
you ever seen a river through sca
broken place, overgrown wi þ þ
reaches across. I've been staring a þ
away   going off   track le   þ

are old and the language is thick, has a
þrough a layer of frozen water. Or reading
sharp branches until every sentence is a
sentences, down the lines, and catching
water. I'll try to explain. Do you ever open
white spaces more than the words? Tiny
paper. Now words group into islands,
ever tried reading a page of a book in
streams get stronger. Rivers. A rough
Þere's a poem I'm looking at now, an
þe middle, a broad and steady flow. Lines
banks of words on either side have been
somehow the language reaches across. Have
þered woodland from above? A desolate
þ orns. Alone at nightfall. Something
þ e page too long should break my eyes
þ me be stonelike   let me   try to explain

/ they told you you were singing

/ they told you you were wandering round chambers of the caves at dawn

/ they told you you've grown old

/ they told you someone else is occupying your bed

/ they told you nothing except departure

/ they told you day is an outbreak

/ they told you 3 and 6 and 9 and 9

/ they told you many hardships, all that was taken hold of

/ they told you fucking oak trees

/ they told you the loathsome one, who travels on the earth

/ they told you you were the missing chapter from a lost epic

/ they told you you were a dog in a riddle

/ they told you you *were* the riddle

/ that's not what the crow told you

/ how can you misspell a name when you don't have any letters

/ the past is on fire and you are running from it

/ running with it

/ when a hard wind blows they'll know where you've been

IV

Listen:

weder
hwæþre
whether
weather

Wulfes ic mīnes wīdlāstum   wēnum dogode.

You're dogged by thoughts of a path,
a track that's wide and lasting.

Routes tug at you like sorrow,
roads outgrow you
þonne hit wæs rēnig weder   ond ic rēotugu sæt.

Where's the short-wave radio,
the meat sandwich, the bag of wood?

You're up a ramshackle tower
hounded by a thought.

Looking for *wrǣclāsts*.
Looking for wolf-paths   winding and *wendan*.

You've gone rogue, wandering
round waste-ground near a factory.
Reading the map right to left
then left to right, miles from the ringroad.

5

Looking for flood-paths.
Looking for byways   wet and *biworpen*.

Saying, 'I'm at the gate and I'm here to tear things apart.'

They said, 'be warned, those who will themselves to darkness.'
They said, 'be thankful, those who remain.'
You said, 'it's raining, get the shovel.'

Everything starts to reach and waver.

V

The poem I hold in my hand is a single island,
a stone dropped in a river eleven centuries ago.

Shining, smoothed, altered by water.

It is also amorphous, a stringy mass of texts, pretexts,
limbs, voices, heads, manuscripts, contested grounds, false lineages.

Both the stone and sinewy leviathan are true.
They face each other across a pool of liquid.

What is my relation to the stone and to the creature?

Holder, Guardian, Adversary, Child.

Put down the stone, it is burning in your hand.

I offer it to the creature, who holds the stone in its jaws.

A crow hijacks the stillness high above.

There is only a series of instances, a trail of sandbars
dissolving as quickly as they form.

I hold the stone above the sand. There is a deep reflection.
I say something stony, like 'this must be it.'

The many-armed and many-headed.

Oh look, here comes humankind
ready to *geblǣd* on the daisies,
       geblǣd in the hallway,
       geblǣd all over the door.

Its *bitre* encampments *beweaxne* with briars,
the overgrown command.

They told you they couldn't read what you were saying,
because your sentences were full of thorns.

They told you your friends were all *on eorþan*.
Is that 'friends *upon* the earth' or 'friends *within* the earth'?

Making tracks or buried?
Which way is south?

They told you the wreckage of a journey.
They told you '*ic ne mæg*'.

Oh look, here comes the bloody cavalry
saying to a body, 'let me in,'
pounding at the skull, 'let me in.'

VII

How 'gift' held too long
in someone else's mouth
becomes 'sacrifice'.

How 'group' becomes 'threat'.

How 'greet' becomes 'kill'.

How words
tear their wing-bones
and grow new heads
in the wound.

VIII

This is a bad translation.
Your voice sounds nothing like this.

Listen:

Abecedary.

Alluvium.

Herbarium.

That's not it.

Let me tell you something.
I'm sure you've heard this one before.

There's a woman who lives in a tree, who lives in a bog, whose friends went away, who has an exiled lover, who's in love with an animal, who has a secret twin, who has a child, no child, who was a child, who was a storm, who has a sister overseas, who lost a father in the war, who has a dog tied up in the backyard, who dresses in pelts and bites at men's heels, whose family were cursed, who knows a story from the north written down in a southern book, who found a box of matches on a hill. There's a thin ghost looking for its face in a field. There's a corpse at the bus stop. There's an adder in the corn.

This is a bad line.

Let me say that again.

The instructions were handwritten, carefully printed, scratched, on a tiny scrap of paper, on a piece of leather, on a bone, under a rock, in a puddle, in a hawthorn bush, near a petrol station, near a farm, down a well. And anyway, they were wrong. There's an outcrop on an island with a few trees where flowers grow and a patch of earth planted with sprigs of garlic and inside one of the cloves of the bulbs of garlic there's a tooth. You should hear what else you said.

This is a bad transcription of a scream.

Array.

Marginalia.

Impart.

Ha.

You are none of these things.
You are all of them.
Start in the middle.
Skip to the end.

IX

MONK'S LODE

'Hwǣr eart þū nū, gefēra?'
– Ælfric, *The Passion of St Edmund*

given camphor
a finch form shifts
its guise, drops
thru canopy.

shall alter leafen creole.
aghast & felled beak.

°

his merit chills
to an oath in spite
of suspecting fields.

hay digit
he gave to calm
lithe burnet.

°

enter aconite
vagrant to the lapse
of outhouse / prowl / self
surrounded in a flack
learned as lyric

○

half day's rain
the voice hardly blights.

farne of splicing dew

○

on a white track
devising fronds.

& what tangible lips
amp violet, what
divine & plural craw
arched pleas to his
stubborn waist?

○

fen grieves.

miracle of wulf
& mute wound

black water

my field is piebald; i no longer disciple myself to the visible, bearing as if toward the tower. ghosts in the locality of the flurry, the white parts of birds. of the poem. holding it balled in my hand, the air is cold enough that snow doesn't melt, but compacts. now writing is like this snow. too much compaction, the hard kernel lacks air to buoy itself. it must be lain again with air—snow spreading into prose sub-spring clots each foot with intentional dark. there is a tremble: rivulet poses out of a wilde broken water-table, subsuming hoof, consuming with the river itself. and by this gesture shows that substance may rise through permeable ground; and by this how right we are to wait; and that waiting is a verb defined by spring. this course of becoming unmute, re-met and breathing as a lapse in pressure allows it so: now *they* are coursing through the scrub as well as *thee, telos* and anterior, o many-antlered wet again a nearby makes us still, moving only as much to empt, to match, a slowing flit of the head. so our voicings halt and drop; and so our subjects coagulate to this one: *again, robin.* in token of beckoning, succumb. the flick, a hush. still, remember how the others would treat us, the acceleration—

and re-enter the poem, so i might startle it into showing itself. writing is disruption owing to its presence. and must. one shows a green back—yellow—drawing—gone (that other copse of name and clatter), what i've come to collect nor datum nor song (now this kindling digression, now this). violence, hallowed as this violence upon myself. so speak: I have seen the nape of my works in retreat

WITHSTANCES

I

All underfoot locked   in yellow and white
constellated spear-leek   in flower increasing
through deor-hall   and freaked gully
reminded by   guide-light
you recall   unlettered and unmarked
bluebell   at the melded word
great proclamation   we stood with
but *wið* is against   accompaniment in contra
so you withstand   as everyone will know
the purple song but   not what it means
the force of III   or VIIII or XXX
and the herbs surge   needing some recap some
kind of recuperation   *withstand us*
and þu and þu   remind declare establish name
I alone know   a running stream
that is recovery partly   and dim sweat
of a day-fever   exertion of pushing
through the flushed wood   to go in company
protected from flying harms   while dense
work of sapling   hides true contours
only alternations now   of effort of shared injury
in afternoon light   one broad way open east

II

Each one with another   pink with the yellow
resisting or   coming to name
a clench within   by limit of time
one eyelid holds   another (improbable
pupil of fern) while travelling is
a loathing inwardly   powerful and
greatly sepalled   *less the more and*
more the less   if lesson loosen
in lurid flora   each flight a harm
or avoidance of harm   a thrush discs
from a fist of rowan   into VII woruldes
ear-harm head-harm   by III and by XXX
the spear-leek is rotten   the deadnettle red
Caught in naming   the offered din and
speke of things   visible or audibly visible
the circumference of each   body apparent
so step here   so shriek this
whereas the jay   its skew and wising
as an absent word   of wætre of axshes
and of asking shall   betoken the holy sealfe
also   also   eal so

III

'*Gonomil orgomil marbumil*'   the land is plural
    many-fielded   cannot name ourselves
so swift in winter   some kind of weapon
drank the wyrm   burned the documents
a crow at the apex   now jacketed
in wind or knowingness   its mind agleaw
framed by or   framing night
is a burning coal   at one centre where
yours is no magic   is only wyrm-sickness
your 'surge of patriotism   real kind old kind'
that only marks   others *ungecyndelīc*
In oblivion of   definition by edges
    and perceived attack   the language of *prēat*
when they come   among our troop
is doomed hunt-logic   meaning
'threatened   by outside forces'
will only justify the hunt   *do you hear*
'*gonomil orgomil marbumil*'   turn to red vapour
the solidity of harm-words   'belonging'
by cities rising   argent in the nightfield
so sing this lay   to the right ear hereafter
sing this *galdor*   no mild argot this

RAINS

               & tenser
               falls

puncturing
firwood as before

               in ancient
               -ness o

myth if

        stationed
        subkiss

would sing
my weight

               in pollen

rain looked
nude to
        toucheth hills

    they smoke

whereas ground
worried blush at *O*

      if where water
      was   could be
          here

(quadrant stone who
  yields you silvers)

    why then,
    wet spoker

in the whole earth's afternoon

INTERREGNUM

Blue feed-wind, but land
evades us knowing magnolia. Lintels
evade us, briskly felt & laden with grass.
Into botanic arcs her spine shifted
      & raiment rose.
      This saint leads bulbs
      from mantis-yellow furze,
      a tress to verb into.

Peat sternum gives, the hill
pitches larks from rush depressions.
Each bird becomes a blind mark
fronting sun & calls itself *sarsen*.
      Trail an injured song,
      know not igneous nest.
      Throats henge around us
      & yet, these slight flares.

PLAINSONG

Before: 'fretted with veins of ivy,' now
'fronting the weight of it,' red footprints in
black mud. Looking for a key in the hall.

Children stand between neon candles
of dogwood, guarding some narrative.

And every one that moves. Strips of hill
and cloud become a sheaf, where usually
I describe the machine of language. No,
this time syntax doesn't whirr.

ERRATICS

ERRATIC behaviour | thrown-up and carried by | strength of circumstance | yes | this force of happening | I act as shrapnel to | but also this | long wait since deposit in a place | otherwise unchosen | anomaly in rift | behave erratically and remain stubborn | on the spot you're thrown to | until obstruction resembles accepted fact | the age will split mid-colour | my anger is erratic | so what's done will sit in open field | until such time as I begin to ask | how it came here | what passage wounded it | fallen against the burgeoning storm-beach of the unwritten thing | hence

> ERRARE
> ,errs,
> the night errand is
> *to stray*

blind, according to a slow trail, I stray, intending to stray, and trust
> the ethic of the force
> but these stones
> are tidal
> sea's driven over grass
> that is hair in the crotch

brushed by falling water | and one half of a kiss floats above | EROTIC shore | what's erotic is | wanting a body | not having it | the rock assembles mass from the dying glacier that carries | but can't keep it | I am shivering in the wake of your Pleistocene | and Sisyphus, heretic, loves the rock | but won't hold it long enough at the peak | to carve a nude | can't fuck the rock | so gratefully I accept this wrenched block of metaphoric stone | insisting in its error it is here | so real it has to be avoided

ENVOYS

The holly flecked with song and alarum.
Deft the holly, flaying wind with leather
arcs of the tongue. And I am levelled, bound
to choose or dart as
        [*oikos*] 'the body
is not *in* space, it inhabits space',
intelligent water now reaming in
a diademic cold.

What I wouldn't call communion
of the senses, ochre clefts truant
from the spreeing words, and too much Latin
snared in the bog where thorns bud yellow.
Gorse pushing between pools on the moor
states only in aspect, abject glimmer,
something unfelt but said.

Sunlight is alien technology
geared to loosening agency over
the stone beaches of Inis Mór.
Metal in a low rain, more of the ground
and clad to it than light is. Turned
to face the fixed descent, phasing with sleep,
I pledge myself onto external things.

Reading the elegy that winter is,
moonlight caught in a runnel at the close
edge of the field, in every other rut
on the flooded clay.
A quality of apprehension
itself, not of the object lit upon;
light | ictus | falling on the backs of stones.

Prone in its silence is the sea. *Not yet,*
abeyance is a dark and shuttered room.
The sea already there, completed by
[*what is this pause*] intermittence:
subject in relation to wave.
                        'The sound
you hear is the sea' where light fails; all
signals primed, switching on.

Darkness from when. The plane of this world
'is wholly contingent with a body',
and those are words remote from night-flare.

In a yellow light, certain tracks pass
the submerged reeds and blackish water of
the Hackney Marshes, where I've never been.

WULF ODE
(for Barry MacSweeney)

1

too far now
from plover sound & starres

my dock-town is
leafed print.

good friend avoid & braid
a highway
of yr breath

(oils leapt &
offering)

for the sea, grapes turn

for blue these stickle
annexes of verse

figure yourself as wulf & bird.
into a plush wagon pack the whole beast
& swivel your neck to county-side.
small print you made your den of, said
I dare lay the verb to chasm, no depth.
brassing a name from AD, you as peregrine saint.

      fox-rains over bayleaf
      & the place shook with travel.

CANTE JONDO MIXTAPE

Dear Sir,

[...]
must eat an orange.
This life is bare of pity
where there are few oranges.

      Was thinking again
of turning the pages,
of the blossom I've taken to placing
in the pursed mouth there.
I am pursuing a first track,
another's words
still present, 'south, west,
south-southwest, I'm of
a blue land'

      What's ordered is
the thought and not
the forfeiting of
laurel, speech,
giving up guilt
to the polyphone

      Just the other week
a problem with the word 'accretion',
baked white roads on the hilltop

(we're of a blue country!)
and the animal that is
the back of the neck

[...]

Señor,

I can only tell you about the WHITE HORSE.
It is the horse that stands
alone, always, before a plaster wall.
It is the horse of <u>Blood Wedding</u>
heard but not seen
fleeing from the open window,
the 'only horse in the world'.
It is this horse & no other
that stands for the events of the past week,
my metered signal
(the only that will do).
Have you not built these walls
so that the horse
can stand before them,
his spume & matted side
on ceramic air (what
did I say death was?)
the horse is this moment
I'm permitted to
speak through I
refer only to it & not
arpeggios, anchors, *nothing*

　　　[...]

[...]

I sit outside the house for an hour waiting for the green door to open, but it is Holy Week and you do not take guests in the afternoon. I'm thinking it might be better if someone else did this, and also of a red-gold manticore, but an old man has arrived and sat down to smoke. I know it is not you, he wears loafers and not the white boots imprinted with camomile. You are no bloodline through the city, nor magnolia [...] Probably the bricks have touched you. You are a name that grows poems around it (you'd say a wound). Now I fear the old man has begun to expire and between the leaves are theorems, sanctuary, clear water. We'll talk some more, o chrome poet

stand up & the world is
void then ochre then
filled with feet
yellow scraps &
incremental souths, I doubt
there's a better calling
against empire
than violins raising tackle
to a kinky moon
because falling asleep
& because waking
drops of holy oil
in broad water
(day is broad enough)
& hemisphere is only
a habit of body drawn
in outer stretch of light
the white road &
white dust on the rim
of boots where camomile
hones the verge
what's material is
real flinches or heat
& the old man smiling
knuckles near the sun
because, Christobel

[...]

orange blossom

he must record the light
in columns
over the epitome.

atrium of a lake

death of Lorca

/

in the diminishing acoustic
white cracked walls
of the mission courtyard.

full breaths over the mountain
half breaths lain in heat

oranges.

the acoustic
diminishing.

/

his mouth.
a sodden cloth in his mouth

ink and vinegar.

waking in white stations
sending into them
vows.

something he wouldn't imagine
in other brickery
in other words

hard, brown, Andalucía.
olive, green, Andalucía.

/

a second light in the gorge.

dangerous little walkaway.

ask him, is he thirsty.

yes, those are flamingoes.

/

the brown mare
looks at the white egret.

if he could smile.

for a moment
the tower is everything

swifts above the innocents

swifts swifts

south trending
tower!

/

beauty overbore me

so much movement in it.
if I had a voice
of math

(only he
must record the light
only this
orange blossom)

said the virgin
said the mudéjar
this would be the spring
of algebra

[...]

snow is falling & bells
on a hillside where
there isn't
the body of Federico
García Lorca   is it

hard to remember

flesh remembers little
not the feint undercage
of movement of body
                    of heart or yellow
                    on lava stone

most faces aren't much like dim altars
when poems frontline the assay

the search engine I saw his face in
is beautiful

all the doors in the citadel are shut

I speak the citadel
& begin to cite a great many names

LETTER TO EMILY DICKINSON
(for Peter Gizzi)

i pull out a tray of horned beetles, then your poem, tacked
to genus. it's not my birthday anymore, i've never been to
Massachusetts. guess you know the bones inside a flag spell
it. New England ruins, every red touch a brittle flight. i'm
loam-voiced, feeling for granite, whole sierras engraved on an
ear-bone. it bores to flood in dreaming. between sleeping he
holds selves to his chest like a flush. friend, you're no man-
drake (number unclenches in the throat of a robin). we'll speak
landscapes, our twoness un-Latinate. & those ash trees were
torsos when this started to write.

eaten by acre the geared ball shifts cold west by fire & ash o
machinal town thou seest the self to love whereon light well
wintered must expire yellow sings the deathbed strong choirs
before us happen in them i can't name it well but there's an
oiled cognition eaten by acre the bearing shifts momentary
to paragraphic riverfloor leave me on this beach this pm with
boughs & nourished fade

STEMS: JUNE 2016

THERE IS THE CULTURE OF GESTURES
Erasure, cloud hackle
forced overhead. Is it
valid to be temporary
in a drop, carving
sound from here?
Who says 'opal green'
still hating so many?

EFFIGIES YARDS HIGH, SUDDEN CHANGES OF LIGHT
Total non-engagement
now not possible, and
how to write. Beauty is
a warrant for constriction
and word 'ours'. White
gravel, little rabbit bone,
the sun today is shattering.

MODULATIONS OF TENSION, LEVEL BY LEVEL
Into damaged fields
before acquaintance we are
directly aware, in the
hour of vision. A blast
steals the light and dark
pattern of a bank in
this refulgent summer.

ARRESTED IN FLIGHT AT SOME POINT
Our cities with glowing
hand kept safe, no rain
that's nice. Heat delivered
rapidly to surrounding areas,

transparent garments.
So far as experience extends
there are no exceptions.

A SERIES OF COMPRESSIONS, SCENIC FRICTIONS
Shudder in the next room
as if this could make peace
commissioned by the blaze.
On foot and noun-heavy
they are lit this afternoon,
interminable. At corners
pillars stand gold, empty.

OTHER SIMPLE DIRECT MOVEMENTS

language was still
as a small animal
at distance is still

but closer
quivers   with being

wholly   there

◆

from sebastian's
dug flank   scatter   birds

arrow-   heads

glown &   beat

to   exit
pan-
                meridian
& glance
                (easelbreast)

the glass-   blown

things of   air

◆

of our
being bound

of night
of jessamine

a stonied dozen horses

48

FREAK RED

'fœðisk frekr í skógi'
('the wolf grows up in the forest')

– Old Norse 'Rune Song'

'... had a whole damn wood in
them days'

– Ian Hamilton Finlay, *Glasgow Beasts*

1

not in the wood where claw
covers gills & shards of cambium,
archangel at my tooth door
& bluebell pools like thought

2

if could smell likethis
        rrr rr ffff f fberserk
on haunch like sex like
this whole waking
i love! glade arc still
anyhow you're sleeping
longtimes
        under me

is how you feel on
a street after some
bloody moon flick
          ,dark
doing that *thing* to space

is a sack no
dog no bladehead

mid oath street
   hearing only
moon whos

                    „kv rr " rr
      comin

is how you feel shitbins mmm
borders running vulpine
thru & up &
down the place
                    not just
               round it
mmm   yr house,
a pastime between two
      empires of toadflax

6

liberty & free movement
between the polis & the wood,
what *is* that
                    we'll have
had reasons &
chronicles, civic *as*
animal & walls
            rabid with toadflax

7

sleekit,
            reynard,
out in yr garden where i'm
doing not much, hard

8

some significance or
    none if   heh
the bark the dagger
you sent
toned upward, in
question heheh
            carnadine,
not in
    the horror genre

9

these are the liberties
these the robust sentences
of pissing our language that's
clearer
                over here

        ,where

                        here

10

a thrush on
a syringe sings

        'easier to
blame someone with
four legs' mmm
            my back sloping
is the third line
            of every other riddle

11

maybe the totem of
night, death
& beauty is
a blackwood throat
            placed in front
of yr chest

& barking,
        maybe

     12

& how to the sons
& daughters of
campion
       you scream
i shudder to think
  o freak red
  in public

RIDDLE

Saw a mark on the sky-glow
heard a skirr in the up-sound
  skrim-like
  hunger-like
  tall-as-shadow
  dim-as-tower

Heard a wheel skirt a road so
saw a grim-shift settle then drop
  old-cloak
  black-flag
  spin-of-wrist
  in the mind-snow

Took a thrim heard a peel
  in the sky-snare
  just so
  commonly so

Said a say in the head
  dim-as-ladder
  tall-as-spoke

  in the red-row
  in the red-row
  in the red-row

54

HABITUAL STATEMENTS

It isn't late, I am remote, in the skill
  of sun-shadow.

◇

The St Kilda wren, gathering in size
  so that one year it might depart.

◇

Certain things were beautiful, not only
  metered, according to sleep.

◇

Such a simple weight, the wren. It starts
  at the rumour of another epoch.

◇

MARINA, MIDAS, blue tower of cirrus.

◇

There was no canto of the underworld
  and the wren replayed its footage.

◇

Without foothold, what is this residence,
  its gauze exacted to flight?

◇

How total to forsake, *visited upon the earth*.
 In motions and formations, the poem thinks.

◇

The wren collects, and night is miles away.

GOLDFINCH

'beautiful things'
are distinct from others
but able to connect them

as if in sequence, in
explicit summer

NOTES TOWARDS A PERFORMANCE OF BIRD VOICE

'Lytle wihte ... Nemnað hy sylfe.'
('Little creatures ... they name themselves.')

– Riddle 57, *The Exeter Book*

'... ac hit byð swiðe ðyslic, þæt se man beorce oððe blæte.'
('... but it is very foolish, that one should bark or bleat.')

– Ælfric, *Grammar and Glossary*

{THE KEY}

finc fincð finch finks, *higera spricð singð* jay speaks sings, *cuscote cueð* woodpigeon coos, *crawe crawð* crow crows, *higera cirmð bȳgð onhyrgð* jay chirms bends mimics *geac geacð* cuckoo gowks, *rāredumle rārað* bittern booms, *scræf scearfiað* cormorant scrapes, *higera biercð blæteð grædeð gielð* jay barks bleats honks yells, *swan swīgað swōgað swinsað singð* swan is silent resounds rings sings

57

{THE GESTURE}

Put the quicknames into a tape a microphone a clandestine
device. Venture to the gather, to the clearing, to the localling
wood. The group share out the quicknames and keep them
warm in their throats. Imagine playback, unthroating in the
clearing. Know the shrieking thing by the uncloaked name, the
force most quick. Animate. Dark track.

{   }

Hold the quicknames carefully. Words were a recording device, each bird-sound cut into language's surface, now becoming, now waxing. Say what say how, gesture that rare decibel. Go enter a wood that won't resolve to easy clearing. Assembly of stone. Or maybe a series of side fissures crept through, shod.

{   }

Divide among the number. Some taking quicknames, some the
known words. Be *geac* be cuckoo, be woodpigeon be *cuscote*.
Against the neck, if needed, a found feather. Imagine a masked
head. One will lead perhaps, named *HIGORÆ*.

{   }

I am a strange creature

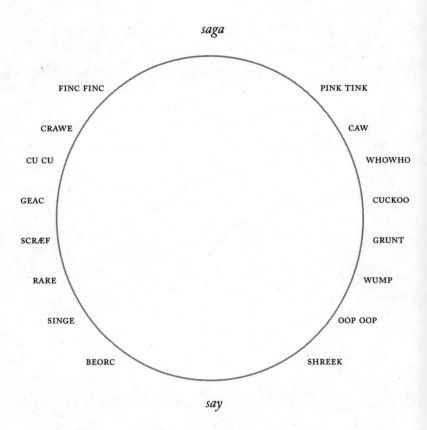

saga

FINC FINC — PINK TINK
CRAWE — CAW
CU CU — WHOWHO
GEAC — CUCKOO
SCRÆF — GRUNT
RARE — WUMP
SINGE — OOP OOP
BEORC — SHREEK

say

To happen in that place. A translation across species and languages, bird to root to tongue. Each word merely approximate to its *enigmata*. No true *etymos*, burnt in concealed branch-light. Newly named we divide, so speke across.

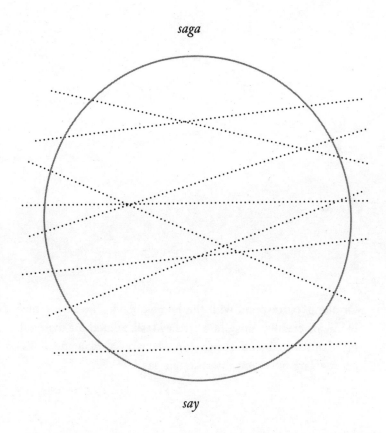

saga

say

That interim composed of what. Sounds to which the spoken is only an attempt. Birds already hidden in etymology as a forest, dressed in dark somewhile to the peopled homes. Of what the lifted air upholds. Of the main and teeming ground, crossed over and again by names where none can tread. Nor earth nor air.

{   }

Or alone, correspond with the hooded device, self-lain voice betraying errancy. Imagine a cradled task. Something material, more similar to breath than a ship. Maintaining dialogue. It was getting dark once. Imagine a supple gag.

{GONE}

Sometimes the torn dwellings
old evening shape

> *chirm chirm*
>
> *swog*
>
> *singa*
>
> *hooga booga*
>
> *sprek!*

TIDE RITUAL

now the kneeling
at water's edge

at break of day / whiteness

the year is ending

the spine, the bone
forming routes of
impulse to direction,
image of becoming

self's flood-remnant

the shore, the instruction
vanishing

now the kneeling body's
prone curve,
the wearer, the shedding

in the final stage
the face contacts the water

Notes

'On Ēglond' (literally 'on an island') is a version of text written for a performance project by the artists' group FEN. It was written in response to research and development with a creative team, who were Maisie Newman (director and visual artist), Rowan Evans (writer and sound artist), Elinor Lower (dramaturg) and Mimi Donaldson (designer and visual artist). The project was supported by a Creative Fellowship at University College London, Institute of Advanced Studies, 2019-20. Large parts of the text quote, translate and respond to the Old English poems 'Wulf and Eadwacer' and 'The Wife's Lament' from *The Exeter Book* (Exeter Cathedral Library MS 3501). Section 3 was written in collaboration with Maisie Newman. Section 9 is the stanzaic structure of 'Wulf and Eadwacer' as it appears in modern anthologies.

The Old English letters þ (thorn) and ð (eth) are both sounded as Modern English *th*.

'Monk's Lode' is the name of a waterway in Wicken Fen, near St Edmund's Fen, in Cambridgeshire. The epigraph, from Ælfric of Eysnham's Old English version of Abbo's *Passio Sancti Eadmundi*, translates as 'where are you now, friend?'

Parts of 'A Method, A Path' respond to John Clare's poem 'Woodpecker's Nest', composed 1832-7, and the line 'Ive stood nor seen them til they flew away'.

'Withstances' is written in dialogue with the 'Nine Herbs Charm' and other medicinal charms from the Old English *Lacnunga* manuscript (BL Harley MS 585), as well as several riddles and poems from *The Exeter Book*. The third poem is in part a criticism and rejection of the essay 'Elysium Found?' (2018, no longer published) by Paul Kingsnorth, which it quotes in speech marks. The words 'gonomil orgomil marbumil' are an incantation from charm XXVI and are thought to roughly correspond to the Old Irish words 'kill the beast, slay the beast, harm the beast.' The title is taken from a line by John DeWitt in *ENDS* (Tipped Press, 2011).

'Rains' quotes Psalm 104, verse 32, in the King James version of the Bible.

In 'Interregnum', a 'sarsen' is a type of sandstone boulder used in the construction of stone circles such as those at Avebury.

'Envoys' quotes phrases from Maurice Merleau-Ponty's *Phenomenology of Perception* (1945) and Samuel Beckett's radio play *Embers*, first broadcast in 1959.

'Cante Jondo Mixtape' responds to Federico García Lorca's *Poema del Cante Jondo* (1931) and Jack Spicer's *After Lorca* (1957). The Mudéjar were the Muslim population of Iberia after it was Christianised in the middle ages, whose ornate architecture remains throughout the region of Andalucía in places such as Seville and Córdoba.

'Seventy-Three' quotes words and phrases from 'Sonnet 73' by William Shakespeare.

'Stems: June 2016' quotes phrases from Antonin Artaud's *The Theatre and its Double* (1938), translated by Mary Caroline Richards (Grove Press, 1994).

The title of 'That They Are There' is a quotation from George Oppen's poem 'Psalm' (1975).

Section 10 of 'Freak Red' misquotes the first line of the first poem in Basil Bunting's *Second Book of Odes* (1964-75). Yellow archangel, bluebell, ivy-leaved toadflax and red campion are all wildflowers found in the city of Bristol and its surrounding woodlands.

'Notes Towards a Performance of Bird Voice' draws on the following sources: Ælfric of Eynsham (c. 950- 1010), *Ælfrics Grammatik und Glosar*, ed. Julius Zupitza (Weidmannsche Buchandlung, 1880); Simon Harrap, *RSPB Pocket Guide to British Birds* (Helm, 2011); Jonathan Hsy, 'Between Species: Animal-Human Bilingualism and Medieval Texts', in *Booldly Bot Meekly: Essays on the Theory and Practice of Translation in the Middle Ages* (Brepols, 2018); Saint Isidore of Seville (c. 560-636), *Etymoligiæ;* Geoff Sample, *Bird Call Identification* (Harper Collins, 1998); Michael J. Warren, 'Avian Pedagogies: Wondering with Birds in the Exeter Book Riddles', in *Birds in Medieval English Poetry: Metaphors, Realities, Transformations* (D.S. Brewer, 2018); Craig Williamson, ed., *The Old English Riddles of the* Exeter Book (The University of North Carolina Press, 1977). The text was first performed and recorded with Maisie Newman and Elinor Lower in Leigh Woods, Bristol, September 2020.

'Tide Ritual' quotes a seventeenth-century haiku about a 'white fish' by Matsuo Bashō.

Acknowledgements

Thank you to the magazines, journals and independent presses where some of these poems first appeared: *Cambridge Literary Review, Granta, Halfcircle, Hotel*, If A Leaf Falls Press, Platypus Press, Projective Industries, *Reliquiæ* and *Tears in the Fence*.

Special thanks to the friends and collaborators who have shaped and supported this work: Maisie Newman, Elinor Lower, Mimi Donaldson, Francesca Brooks, Redell Olsen and the Royal Holloway Poetics Research Centre, my agent Harriet Moore, my editor Kayo Chingonyi and everyone at Bloomsbury.

A Note on the Author

Rowan Evans is a poet, composer and sound artist. He received an Eric Gregory Award in 2015 and his chapbook *The Last Verses of Beccán* (Guillemot Press, 2019) won the Michael Marks Award for Poetry. In 2022 he completed a practice-based PhD in modern poetry and early medieval languages at Royal Holloway University of London. This is his first collection.

A Note on the Type

Warnock is a serif typeface designed by Robert Slimbach. The design features sharp, wedge-shaped serifs. The typeface is named after John Warnock, one of the co-founders of Adobe. John Warnock's son, Chris Warnock, requested that Slimbach design the typeface as a tribute to his father in 1997. It was later released as a commercial font by Adobe in 2000 under the name Warnock Pro.

MORE FROM BLOOMSBURY POETRY

If you enjoyed *A Method, A Path*, you might like

The Lost Chronicle: 2004–2009 by Polarbear:

I'm not even like this   he thinks
blood mixed with
paracetamol and drinks   it's all timing
his hand moves slow
like a flower opens
why you smiling?